Cover Design: Haymaker Collective

SIGNIFICAN'T
7 Invitations To Heart Revival

Be More.

TerrenceTurman.com

Table of Contents

Acknowledgements and Dedications

First and foremost, I want to acknowledge God and all of His vast mercy in my life. The lessons I share here would not be possible without His grace.

Secondly, I want to thank my loving wife Brittany for always being my biggest support. Thank you for patiently watching me stress, rewrite and work through this book with a spirit of love and encouragement. You make me better.

To my friend Kelly Hamilton, thank you for telling me to pick my pen back up. You have always been an encourager for me so I thank you!

To my friend Sharla Carter, thank you for reading and editing my rough draft into proper English as you sat through chemotherapy! You have always been a beautiful person and I believe that even more now!

This book is dedicated to every teacher, coach, minister, family member and friend that has spoken worth into my life. Your value to me cannot be understated. Thank you!

Lastly I acknowledge my weakness before the Lord. If I have written anything henceforth in error, I ask for your forgiveness Father God!

A Call to Worship

In lieu of a traditional introduction, I instead want to call you into worship. I do this because I have written this book primarily as a pastor and my sole purpose is for the reader's heart to be moved not towards an amusement with my words but instead a deeper worship of King Jesus!

With that said, I welcome you to today and to this time of worship. I invite you to open-handedly welcome Jesus and His Spirit into this time with you. Nothing in the pages to come will matter unless He is at the center. In response to that truth, read these words (aloud if you are comfortable) and accept this call to worship.

"But I enter your house
by the abundance of your faithful love;
I bow down toward your holy temple
in reverential awe of you.
8 Lord, lead me in your righteousness
because of my adversaries;
make your way straight before me."
Psalm 5:7-8 CSB

With thanksgiving in your heart throughout your reading,
Let this be a time of worship!

Chapter 1

What is a Heart Revival?

*God, create a clean heart for me and
renew a steadfast spirit within me- Psalm 51:10*

What is a heart revival? Before we answer that
question, I want to start our time together in a peculiar way.
I want to start by telling you a personal story about seltzer
water. Now what comes to mind when you read that
sentence has a lot to do with your own experience. Maybe it
was a thirsty moment at a fast food joint, anticipating your
favorite beverage, but instead what filled your cup was
simply fizzy water impersonating something tasty. Maybe it
was one of those cold remedy seltzers, you know the ones
that promise their new delicious flavor makes them easier to
drink -- only for you to realize even the medicine world can't
be trusted with your feelings. Maybe it's the new fad
commercials we see with the fit people hanging out on a
boat drinking an ice-cold seltzer as if the very presence of
seltzer brings life to the party.

I've had all of those experiences, but my worst
experience was the surprise attack by a beautifully labeled
can of seltzer water I will not name. Let's just say it rhymes
with "ahoy!" Anyway, I remember the day like it was
yesterday. As I walked to the cooler passing many people, I

began to notice many women, mostly in their 20's, enjoying this mysterious beverage that I had never tried but had often seen on the shelves. It felt like I was living in that commercial, surrounded by smiling faces, big gulps and laughs all with this drink in hand. Not wanting to be deceived, I got clearance from a trusted person nearby: "Are those things any good?" She replied quickly with a puzzled face, "You've never had one before? Yes, they are amazing! If you like clear soda, you will love it!" Now with more confidence than ever, I plunged my hand into the icy cooler and grabbed what by the can's design, promised to be a good time full of Mango flavor. With excitement, I ripped the can open and took a big swallow, only to have -- what felt like a millisecond later -- what had just gone down, make its way back up! With a gag and spit, my good time found its way to the nearest trash can. It's a moment to laugh about now and it was a great memory during a long day of ministry training, but it was also the day I decided to never drink seltzer water again......Until l did.

You see, my story with seltzer water didn't end there. There is a saying that I'm not quite sure I believe, but I've been told our taste buds change every so often, and with that comes new foods that meet our cravings. This is usually said when referencing healthier eating, so I'm suspicious that other factors come into play like new diets, health diagnoses and aging bodies. With all those things in mind, people tend to begin making sacrifices and healthier choices as they age and mature. Instead of burgers and fries, we go for a burger and side salad. Instead of sweet tea we order half sweet, half unsweet. We start counting calories and before you know it, a zero-calorie beverage with zero sugar sounds like a great option! At least that's what happened to me. I like to call this moment in our lives, the sanctification process of our diets. Whether we want it to happen or not, it will...by choice or by force.

After making some lifestyle changes to my eating habits, I found myself revisiting that once-bitter beverage for one more tango. This time my approach was different. Number one, I understood that what I was about to drink was not a sugar-filled delight but promised natural flavors that carried their own "sweetness." Number two, I had experience now. I knew what it could taste like so I set my bar lower to give myself room for a surprise. And number three, my purpose was different. This wasn't a wondering curiosity or chasing after a craving. This time, I was denying myself for a higher and better reason. This time, what the drink was made for was exactly *why* I grabbed it. Long story short, what once was bitter and hard to drink has now become my favorite beverage and makes the grocery list every time. No frills and no misplaced expectations. Just a nice cold zero-calorie seltzer to meet me where I am on my health journey.

Now here's the twist. What if I told you that for many Christians, my story with seltzer water has been the consistent struggle with their pursuit of the Christian life and some of its most fundamental principles? These sweet promises of following Jesus seem to come back void and bitter as we grasp for a drink of things like forgiveness, love, reconciliation and many other aspects of the Christian life. We read these calls to walk as Jesus did and it seems impossible after we leave dissatisfied for the 100th time.

Ultimately, our pursuit to live outside ourselves leaves us with a nice gut punch, disrupting any hope we had to be good people who actually live the "What Would Jesus Do" life. Because of this, many are stuck in the tidal waves of lukewarm Christendom. We attend church 1.8 times a month, we give our tithes and offerings most of the year, and then wait for the church to announce all the good things we've done to change the world. Yet I believe deep down, inside the hearts of most people is a desire to try again. We want to live a life of impact that has nothing to do with fame and fortune but instead brings a significance that breaks cycles and leaves a legacy worth remembering. That's why I wrote this little book. To meet you where you are and nudge you not to grow tired of doing good. To be a cheerleader in your race as the Spirit leads you towards your crown that won't perish.

How do I get there?

The question then remains, how do we get there? I'm not sure I have your answer verbatim but I do have an idea in principle! It's the same solution that led me back towards seltzer water and the same one that keeps me drinking them daily. It's asking yourself "your why" and remembering the purpose of pursuing the Christian life in the first place. My "why" for drinking flavored seltzer water is to cut my calories and drink less sugar. I do not choose this because I don't prefer the sugary love I grew up on, but because my family deserves a better me. It is because my health calls for a more "sanctified" diet. That reality invites me daily to pursue selflessness that ironically serves me well in the long run. For the Christian life, that "why" should center on Jesus and His unmerited grace. It should center on making His kingdom now as we wait for the "not yet!" It's accepting the reality that our worlds and spheres of impact call for a more sanctified us! The work of that "why," bitter as it may taste at times, can be like sweet nectar to the soul!

Another principle is understanding we can't live a meaningful Christian life without a daily partnership with God! In so many ways, the modern church has become obsessed with the "Acts" church! We love the worship. We love the intimate community. We love the sacrificial living. We read Acts 2 and subsequently Acts 4 and our hearts long for that same Christian fellowship. We read about Phillip,

Stephen and Saul turned Paul and desire a movement like that where we live. And time and time again, churches are planted promising to be "like the church in Acts." Time and time again, members go from church to church searching for what their last one was missing. Time and time again, pastors and leaders pump out sermon series challenging their churches to be what they read, and where they end up most of the time is back at square one, reading Acts and wondering why their experience is so different. In the midst of that, most of us miss the most important part of that movement 2000 years ago, and that is their consistent submission and reliance on God.

Go back and read the pages of Acts; there is no moment of significance that did not have the stamp of the Godhead and, specifically, the Holy Spirit. John 16 tells us that the Holy Spirit's main job is to make much of Jesus. It's important for us to know that, because His primary means of doing that will be to work in and through the life of Jesus Followers to declare His glory to the world. If we know this to be true, then it makes sense that any approach to multiply our lives and make much of Jesus without the Holy Spirit would eventually fail and fall bitter to our sensibilities. If we truly want to make much of Jesus and live a life that multiplies, then I suggest we all adopt a different approach. It's an approach that carries the namesake of this book but one that puts all of life into perspective. It's an approach that says, as clear as our "why" may be, we will never attain the satisfaction of such living without first acknowledging that we can't do it on our own merit! It is the idea that as we pursue daily communion with God and His purposes while embracing selflessness, we are pursuing a signif**ICan't** life!

Now obviously, I made up this word! I wouldn't imagine those who write dictionaries will be lining up to add it to their ever-growing list of words, but I challenge you to add it to your daily rhythm. I find it quite fascinating that right there inside the word significant, we see "I Can't." As a former athlete who has heard all the customary "you can't spell this word without that word" speeches over the years, I find that my brain now has a hard time *un*seeing the possibilities. For that reason, do not be alarmed by the apostrophes littered throughout this book. They're intentional. I placed them there to remind us that as we read, we must do so understanding our need for God's help. My goal is not to write you a list of moral suggestions, but to invite you deeper into life transformation. My goal is to challenge you to ask God daily, "Where can I be *significan't* today? How can I live *significan'tly* different than the world today? Who needs my *significan't* love today? Where do I need to let you be signif*can't* in my life today?" I guess another way of saying that is to echo Paul in 2 Corinthians when he says, "Test yourselves to see if you are in the faith.

Examine yourselves. Or do you yourselves not recognize that Jesus Christ is in you? Unless you fail the test."

So, to get back to answering the chapter's opening question, what is a heart revival? Simply put, a heart revival is when God's people are reawakened to embrace a God-dependent, fruit-bearing life that moves us towards a gospel expression that truly loves God and loves people. It's re-engaging life marked by the "I can't but God can through me" attitude even when we don't enjoy it.

With every invitation in this book, you are invited to join God in sanctifying the diet of your actions for the good of others and for His pleasure. You are invited to embrace life understanding God does the extraordinary through our obedience and dependency. He does this not just in miraculous ways but also in the ordinary decisions, happenings and moments of our lives. In a world that says liberation, joy and peace is found in "doing you", Jesus says "follow me". As we learn to say yes more, we learn to love His way more and as we learn to love His way more, we learn He truly knows what's best for us. When we walk assured in that reality, we can begin to walk in the rest that flows from it.

Meet me at the cooler

Are you ready to explore more about what it means to live *significan't*? Then I invite you to keep reading, but before you turn the page please humor me for a second and join me at the ice cooler. Imagine yourself opening that cooler and at the bottom you spot a nice cold can of seltzer water. Pop that bad boy open, sit back and enjoy some words that I hope meet a thirst that leaves you wanting more!

Ahead for you are seven timeless encouragements that move us towards *significan'tce* and meet us in the crux of our weakness and dependency on God! Each chapter is meant to simply nudge you to consider the idea of *significan'tce* for your own journey. I've chosen to give these seven invitations because I believe within them are doorways of growth to all facets of life.

I've written this book to be versatile in its reading. It is just short enough to be read in one sitting, hopefully with much prayer as you journal in the margins. Or you can savor it for a week sip by sip, asking God to meet you right where you are in your journey of significan'tce! Regardless of how you choose to take it in, if you finish this little book with a heart of reflection, then my job is done and I will trust the Holy Spirit to do the rest! God Bless and Happy Reading!

Chapter 2

Forgive Undeservingly

"For if you forgive others their offenses, your heavenly
Father will forgive you as well. But if you don't forgive
others' your Father will not forgive your offenses."
-Matt 6:14-15

Now, where I want to start is at the end. I find it
appropriate as we look at forgiveness and its possibilities
that we revisit the moment where Jesus seems to set the
most impossible example, His forgiveness from the Cross.
After a series of events that included betrayal by a friend, an
unjust trial, a beating that left his back skinless and the
excruciating experience of crucifixion, Jesus still knew
forgiveness. We find His words in Luke 23:24, as Jesus cries
out to His father, a plea of forgiveness for the very ones least
deserving of His mercy. Without a doubt, Jesus forgave
undeservingly and that, my friends, is our example to
emulate.

In a world in which forgiveness, mercy and
understanding seem lost, a Jesus ethic on forgiveness is the
exact framework we all need. In saying that, I am not naïve
to the difficulty of living out that forgiveness. I mean, we
often have a hard time forgiving ourselves for shortcomings,

so to extend to others what we might not have for ourselves is a tall task. Yet in that reality, we have to believe that Jesus has a better framework. Jesus has a better way!

An undeserved forgiveness is one found by decreasing ourselves in favor of reliance on God. It is a fruit that can only be produced within us when we acknowledge our weakness and His strength. Paramount to this forgiveness and fruit bearing is a Jesus-centered surrender of our wills towards His. What that looks like is a forgiveness from the cross. It's a forgiveness that might be painful. It's one that might be rejected but it may be one that brings restoration.

You've probably heard it said a million times that forgiveness doesn't mean reconciliation. On a number of levels that statement is true. Forgiveness requires one person to move on whereas reconciliation requires both parties to move together. Forgiveness is a state of being; it's a posture towards a person or situation, whereas reconciliation is renewing something for the sake of journeying together. Without a doubt there is a clear distinction, yet I believe as we search the scriptures and the model of Jesus we will find a clear truth. Though forgiveness doesn't *mean* reconciliation, Jesus shows us true forgiveness from His grace and mercy leaves that door wide open.

This type of forgiveness is the kind that blows us away every time we see a family ravished by the evil of sin, tell a killer, "We forgive you." It's the kind of forgiveness that then moves the family to build a relationship with said killer and love him into his old age as he spends the rest of his life in prison. I hope to never face a scenario of that kind but I hope that my commitment to Christ would swell up in the same way. A way that says, what was meant for evil will now multiply much good. To forgive undeservingly is to reflect the immeasurable and unmerited grace God extends to us, to those around us. It's to live outside of ourselves, pursuant of right relationship with others on the merit that God extended right relationship to us freely through the loving, redemptive work of Jesus.

The Risk

Now leaning in can be risky. As we have seen, pursuing this way of life is going to cost us something yet sometimes what it costs are things we didn't know we valued. I attended a men's weekend recently that covered unleashing the inner man God intended us to be. One of the many things I learned was that every decision we make has something to gain but also something to lose. It's often very easy to identify the win and risk of making tangible decisions like job change. For instance if I take the new job, maybe I will find better pay, a new adventure and a fresh start, but if I stay I will keep stability, status quo and predictability. If I leave I risk comfort and security and if I stay I risk not having another shot or simply being bored.

But what about something not so tangible, like the win and risk of forgiveness?

There is no doubt a laundry list of wins we can identify by granting forgiveness so I'm not interested in spending time there. I want to focus on the cost and the question, "What's the risk?"

In facing down the risk of what might seem like an awfully bitter forgiveness, we have the opportunity to dig deep and do the unthinkable. You've heard it said forgive but never forget, but I believe Jesus modeled an ethic for us that says "forget as you forgive." Now before you close this book out of disagreement, let me share what I mean. When I say forget, I understand that we will never truly forget the things that have hurt us most. Those things will be in our memory until we are laid to rest, yet I believe another kind of forgetfulness can exist within us. Just as God promises to throw our sins away in the sea of His forgotten memory, we can do the same in our finite way. In theory, that looks good on paper and doesn't sound like much risk. What that means practically, however, will change the narrative. To live out that type of forgiveness is to find the courage to relinquish our role as the victim, and the birth rights of our pain, accusation and retaliation.

If you've ever been hurt relationally you understand the toil and wrestling that is involved in moving on towards forgiveness. There may have been times when we thought we had forgiven someone, and then a trigger reminds us of a previous hurt. For example, maybe it's a spouse who experienced infidelity but made the commitment to forgive the other and move on in the marriage. Maybe things have been going well for a year and then all of a sudden he or she isn't answering the phone after being late from work. The scenario feels all too familiar as these were the signs of their unfaithfulness before, so without a second thought, that is the reality. When he/she finally returns home 30 minutes later, an argument ensues and before you know it the purpose of the argument has changed. Instead of discussing what happened and reconciling the angst, accusation takes center stage. Knowing it would hurt, the words, "Are you cheating on me again?" brings the room to a new level of seriousness. In disbelief the spouse yells back, "I told you my phone died. How long are you going to not trust me? I thought you said you forgave me; I thought we were moving on. I said I was sorry, what more can I do?" As the smoke clears and no infraction has been found, regret fills the room. One lives in a cycle of shame from a broken past, while the other feels the overwhelming reality that the forgiveness they gave was being exposed as a grab for stability at the most. End scene!

You may know this reality or you may have seen it in a movie but whether reality or silver screen, we see the power and destruction of accusation. We see the ease and comfort we find in retaliation. In one moment, a year's worth of progress left this couple because the risk of a forfeited accusation and retaliation was too much for the spouse who had been hurt before. The truth is, they attempted reconciliation without true forgiveness. One spouse moved forward in better and for worse while the other continued with "you better not make it worse."

Now forfeiting our right to accuse is not a call to be a fool, but a call to be free. It's a call to new mercies every day for those in our lives and around us. It's pleading the case to our fleshly desires and imitating the Christ who intercedes on our behalf, moving the Father to new mercies, not just daily but moment by moment with us (Romans 8:34). In this posture we no longer need to keep a tab from yesterday that piles on frustration. Instead, we get to find our position at the mercy seat of God as the coffee brews each morning. There is a freedom to love and cherish when we let go of what once muddied the waters of joy and relationship. Instead of missing the moments, our posture turns to *making* the moments. The difference between the two is the simple art of forgiveness, the one that forgives and forgets.

With that said, let's visit Jesus back on the cross. Bloody and beaten on our behalf. Spat upon. Carrying the sins of the world we find a man of mythical proportions extending an unthinkable grace towards an inconceivable forgiveness. If Jesus could do it there in that moment, then surely we can find the courage to chase His shadow in this moment! *Significan't* forgiveness is forgiveness undeserved. It's forgiveness unmerited. Give it away!

Prayer

Father God, I thank you for the gift of your forgiveness. I thank you that you saw fit before my life began, to make that reality possible. I want to forgive like you do, Lord. I acknowledge that on my own, I can't offer what you so graciously give freely to all of us. I repent of my hardened heart towards forgiveness at times. I repent of all the times I have refused to even consider the possibility in light of your unmerited grace towards me. Lord, I request that you would meet me where I am weak and be my strength. Give me the capacity to imagine a life where I forgive through your grace and through your love. Allow me to freely give what I so freely receive. Holy Spirit, help me make much of Jesus by the way that I forgive and forget. Help me to exude with your fruit as I offer forgiveness to those who offend me. In Jesus' name I pray, Amen

3 Heart Deep Questions

1) What Did You Hear From God As You Read?

2) What Did You Learn About Yourself?

3) Is There A Step You Need to Take? If So, What Does That Look Like?

Chapter 3

Reconcile Relentlessly

"So if you are offering your gift on the altar, and there you remember that your brother or sister has something against you, [24] leave your gift there in front of the altar. First go and be reconciled with your brother or sister, and then come and offer your gift"- Matt 5:23-24

Reconciliation is at the heart of whom God is. After taking the time to read a little about His forgiveness, we must deal with His heart in which that flows. There can be no reading of the Bible accurately without seeing this posture from God throughout the pages of scripture. From front to back, we see a plan of God that consistently leads towards restored relationships and a reconciled existence. As those who are seeking a *significan't* life, it is imperative that we lead the way in society by being the ones who still value and pursue the path of reconciliation.

In 2 Corinthians 5, Paul teaches us that those who have been commissioned by God carry with them a ministry of reconciliation. In simple terms, Christ followers are those who reconcile. We reconcile in relationships. We reconcile the brokenness around us. We reconcile the sin of our culture. We reconcile as a function of following Jesus.

Making things on Earth as it is in Heaven is what we do. It's the missional life we are called to. Though Paul penned that letter nearly 2000 years ago, its implications are just as timely. The world needs reconcilers.

The Way of This World

In 2020 we saw a world pandemic and racial injustice implode our lives yet the most destructive trend was this continual shift towards a canceling and confrontational culture that has no room for reconciliation. Now to the passersby, my assertion would seem wrong. Words like "unity," "together" and "love" have all trended on social media but time and time again what paraded around under a cloak of reconciliation soon revealed itself to be nothing more than a call to conformity and at its worst, fear mongering. Just ask NBA player and brother in Christ Jonathan Isaac.

During the early days of the COVID-19 pandemic, to the excitement of millions around the globe, we witnessed the return of the NBA. With it, we witnessed moment after moment and commercial after commercial, with messages about unity and strength together. Yet, beyond all that, I believe we also witnessed a tragedy.

If you don't know, Jonathan was the lone NBA player to stand for the national anthem and not wear a "black lives matter" t-shirt during the first round of games deciding to instead use His voice to share a gospel message.

In doing so, he exposed a sad reality about what tends to be true for most mainstream movements in our history: their aim is more about uniformity and power than the actual work of reconciling uniquely different people. Fueled by mutual anger rather than mutual love, they can function more as avenues of retribution and justice rather than tools for deep communal reconciliation. As a result, the victories that are produced can be considered nothing more than partial victories and bandages to the bigger problem because anger and self-gratification must always have an enemy. So when it came to Jonathan, his decision in their eyes was not a solution to be considered but a defiance that needed to be handled accordingly. No matter how much merit his position had, it challenged their "righteous" anger to righteous action and the self-gratifying humanity we are at times just didn't like that.

As hundreds of NBA players and coaches knelt, wearing the "right" shirts seemingly to amplify black voices including Jonathan's, none had the same courage and conviction in making sure his mattered in that moment. Outside of the pointed interview questions, no one stood up and protected Jonathan and his voice. Now, I'm sure they all had their reasons but I suspect a major and maybe even a hidden motivation was that the implications were just too risky for their comfort. It required selflessness that I'm not sure they were ready for.

In hindsight, I do believe Jonathan could have worded his thoughts better. In a world that is continually pushing Christian thought to the margins, it's imperative that we communicate with clarity to rightly portray what is the greatest love of all, the gospel of Jesus Christ. With that said, I think he understood the essential truth that unity in message means nothing without reconciliation in hearts. He understood that no *significan't* change to the realities of our world would ever happen without *significan't* change to the hearts of people and that sentiment would surely rang true in the weeks to come. While the big name companies touted the power of these "moments of solidarity" while raking in the dollars along with it, we saw a different reality play out in the world around us. Our streets, schools, relationships, churches and social media platforms all sounded an alarm that the kneeling, the shirts, the speeches and the commercials as useful as they may be in some small measure just weren't working. The need was much greater.

It still amazes me that in a matter of months, our communities went from a growing and budding display of brotherly love in the early days of Covid to everyone picking a corner and forming separate mobs by mid-summer. We went from sharing our toilet paper and can goods to sharing just how much we despised each other with relative ease.

As I let my mind go back to that night, as a reporter asked Jonathan, "What does religion have to do with kneeling and protesting?" My heart sinks, because in that moment, I realized the hope Jonathan was trying to share had truly been misunderstood as foolishness to the world. The hope of change I had growing in me as a black man at that time was quickly snatched away by the wisdom I knew in the Lord. Ultimately, we were still lost!

Now truthfully, this chapter is not about Jonathan's story and what played out on that day. Instead, his story serves us as a picture of the war that can happen inside of us when faced with the opportunity to live reconciling lives. It shows us what can happen in our own hearts when we choose to walk in anger and allow self-gratifying motives to lead our choices. We can become people more concerned with what's convenient in the moment rather than what's right or best long term. We can become consumed with keeping our peace or getting our way rather than being the peacemakers Jesus calls us to be. We can become people who know God is calling us one way but instead be those that choose our own path for the victory we desire. Instead of seeking to reconcile, we seek to slander, dismiss and dishonor. Instead of reaching for the other person with hope in mind, we push them away with malice, ill intent and cold shoulders. We see problems in this world and throw our hands up rather than throw a hand out to make a difference. Sure, there is some small sense of relief or gratification in those choices but the wins never last because the war within us and around us keeps raging and the anger, rightful or not, lives on to lead our lives.

I don't know about you but this reality has rang true in my life many times. Whether it was with family, coworkers, bosses, friendships or even my marriage, I have allowed a justified anger to be my Jesus and a righteous cause to excuse my sin. I've allowed righteous indignation to tie my hands towards my neighbors in need missing the opportunity to reconcile the brokenness and I imagine I'm not alone in that.

As I reflect on that, I feel my heart longing for another option. I would dare to say despite all the emotional thrill or relief we get from choosing our own way, we actually desire something better. We can see that all of the emotional kneeling, picketing and protesting, as useful as they feel, just haven't produced what we truly desire. But likewise, I would dare to say Jesus has that something better for us. In fact, something *significan'tly* better but only if we are willing to trust and try His narrow and less traveled way.

The Jesus Way

Have you ever tried to reenact a first date? We see it all the time in romantic movies. The guy stops noticing the small things and the girl feels unnoticed, then they reenact their first date and we witness the moment where their romance has a rebound. The date usually takes place at some random park where they split a sandwich 10 years ago and fell in love. The guy in his best effort tries to reproduce every aspect of that night from the time of day to the stranger playing violin for cash. As all the events unfold, she realizes what is happening and then it happens, he drops to one knee and asks the question, "Will you marry me?" She says yes of course and then the movie speeds off to their wedding and a happy ending.

Truth is, we've seen that play out so many times that we have almost become numb to the story's intent and power. If we stripped away all of the "cheese" from those movies in our brain space, we would see the principle of reconciliation in full bloom. In one scene we could witness the state of a relationship move from resentment to restoration.

What if I told you Jesus wrote the book on that scene and did it better? It was early one morning 2000 years ago where Jesus set the standard. On a sandy beach, Jesus made his appearance. In a time when all hope seemed lost, there off in the distance stood the Hope of The World. Jesus was there to make right what had been wronged, except here's the difference: He was the one wronged. See, just off the coast line sat some of Jesus' closest and beloved friends. Primary in the group was Peter. Just about a week earlier, these men had all experienced the traumatic experience of watching their leader, their rabbi and their friend unjustly murdered. On the way towards that death Peter, who happened to be the most zealous of Jesus' followers, became the most cowardly and denied doing life with Jesus to preserve his own. The weight of that decision crushed his spirit and now we find him returning to the only thing that gave him comfort and assurance before, fishing. As he sat in his boat with friends, a voice came from the shore asking if they had a catch. After replying with an emphatic no, the stranger in the distance suggested they cast their nets to the other side. Upon doing so, fish abounded and then it clicked. Soon Peter and the other men found themselves amazed by Jesus in the same way they were years earlier. In the same way He had called them years ago into a loving relationship and purpose, Jesus was there to restore purpose and passion back into His disciples. In spite of the heartbreaking reality of their unbelief and unfaithfulness, Jesus didn't cancel, He extended grace. He reconciled.

On a sandy beach, Jesus set a table with those whom He could have rightly called enemy. Instead He chose to reinitiate relationship. Where the culture might have called for things like avoidance, name calling and shame, Jesus cooked breakfast.

Christ-follower, that is your lane to run in. That is your commission. Your call is to be light, salt and most of all imitators of Christ. To accurately do that, is to faithfully give out what Jesus has faithfully given to you. Just as he met

Peter in his messy life, so too does Jesus meet us every day in ours. He provides our daily portion and forgives our trespasses. He restores our hearts and renews our spirits. Instead of canceling us, He counsels us. Instead of tolerating our relationship, He seeks to transform it.

When we are at the well like the Samaritan woman, He counsels us. When we are repeat offenders like Peter, He counsels us. When we are ones caught in adultery and unfaithfulness, He counsels us. And as I write this and you read it, He counsels us! In that counseling, we find miles of love, joy, peace, patience, kindness, goodness, faithfulness, gentleness and self-control. And in that grace, we've found transformation.

In light of that truth, may we graciously be those who meet others in their trespasses. May Christ's love lead us to be reconcilers in every space we enter for the sake of His Kingdom. As Christ followers, may we fight for what is good but also resist whatever is not true, whatever is not noble, whatever is not right, whatever is not pure, whatever is not lovely, and whatever is not admirable first and foremost in ourselves then unto the world. May we be faithful to pick up truth but never leave grace behind understanding the way of Christ, painfully inconvenient as it is at times, brings significan't transformation. And that my friends is always worth it. Reconcile relentlessly!

Prayer

Father God, I thank you for the truth that is reconciliation. I thank you that this is not an idea that is too far off but very much in the realm of your ability. I want to be a reconciler, someone who brings people and things back together. I acknowledge that on my own I can do nothing, so I humbly ask that you would meet me here. I repent of all the times I've tried on my own or doubted your power to heal. I repent of anytime that I've resisted your nudge to do more and reach across the aisle. With that I ask for your help. Holy Spirit, help me make much of Jesus by the way that I reconcile and build bridges. Help me to exude with your fruit as I pursue relational harmony with those around me. In Jesus' name I pray, Amen

3 Heart Deep Questions

1)   What Did You Hear From God As You Read?

2)   What Did You Learn About Yourself?

3)   Is There A Step You Need to Take? If So, What Does That Look Like?

Chapter 4

Heal Wholeheartedly

*"But he was pierced because of our rebellion, crushed because of
our iniquities; punishment for our peace was on him, and we are
healed by his wounds." –Isaiah 53:4-5*

I was about 5 years old the day my life changed
forever though at the time I had no clue such damage had
taken place. It was a typical Saturday hanging at my house
during this time. My family still lived at my Granddad's
house in a season of transition and per usual, all the cousins
were dropped off to be under his supervision as our parents
went on with their day handling whatever tasks had been
put off during this week. This time, I think it was Christmas
shopping.

I was always the youngest boy in the group with the
next closest being four years older than me so it's safe to say
I was the runt of the litter, always trying to keep up and
always seeing, hearing and knowing more than I should.
Typically, these days were centered around some type of
gaming system. Usually Techmo Bowl and Street Fighter
until somehow the competition came to blows but this day
was different. This day, the star of the show was the freedom
to explore the "adult channels" that were off limits to the

kids. Leading the charge was an older cousin probably around the age of 15 or so who very much knew what lay ahead on those channels.

For context, I grew up in a household in which we had to cover our eyes on the "bad scenes" in movies. We weren't a Christian home at this time aside from the remnant of my mom's religious upbringing but there was still a line for us that was clear and we all knew not to cross it and get caught. Without a doubt, what was going down that day, was a clear violation of what was expected out of the kids in our family. If caught, everyone could expect an old fashioned southern beat down and maybe a week of being grounded.

As the story progresses, we didn't get caught but I sure wish we were because that day was likely a day that deeply formed all of us and not in a good way. As the television began to flip, I became increasingly uncomfortable so I left the room. I just remember not feeling good about what was happening. As I was looking for a place to retreat, I remember the older boys bringing me back into the den and closing the door affectively forcing me to join them in watching the pornography that for some reason was being paid for and on in the middle of the day. By this time, an older girl had been dropped off to hang and she too joined the fray. She was also a few years older and obviously well aware of the material that was happening on that screen.

What should have been a room of kids and teens hanging out playing games or watching the tube turned into a full blown adult movies watch party that quickly escalated into re-enactment. One by one, the boys went into the bathroom and for about a minute would remain in there with the girl and come out. All of a sudden it was my turn and I didn't want to go into the bathroom. I remember standing in the long narrow hallway trying to force my way out but ultimately being pushed in to which I found out what was happening on the other side of the door. To keep this book from crossing a line and maybe becoming too triggering for others, I won't describe what happened but will say, I was never the same afterwards.

That day happened in 1995 and I never spoke of it again until 2014 as I began to explore the possibility to go into ministry. At the time, I was meeting a counselor and had self-identified a long standing addiction to porn dating back to my childhood. After asking questions as to how this could be, I gave typical answers like, I was just a "mannish" child. This of course was the language of others in times I presented behaviors that seemed too becoming for my age as a result of what I had been exposed to. I said that I'd always had a lust problem for as long as I could remember but as a trained counselor knows, my answers were victim language, there was something deeper that maybe I didn't realize which was the case. He began to ask me questions that ultimately led to the memory of that day and without hesitation, He said, "Terrence, that was sexual abuse". With shock and anger, I immediately began to defend my family and honestly my manhood. I was nobodies' victim and my family loved me and never would hurt me in such a way, besides we were all just kids.

As he allowed me to sit for a while, he gently walked me through how abuse has many faces and many motivators and scenarios. He told me kids abuse kids quite often and many times neither child sees themselves as an abuser or a victim because there was no malicious intent. He pointed out that the porn addiction I reported is likely very well linked to the wound of that day that had gone unseen, untouched and unnamed for over 20 years. As I gathered myself, we began to again walk through my story and before you know it, multiple memories began to flood back, there was a sleepover with a friend that repeatedly touched me inappropriately as we lay in bed, there was witnessing sex playout between the older kids of the neighborhood, there was the hidden porn stash I found in a relatives closet as I was trying to find something else and so much more I won't write here because frankly, I haven't processed it all yet.

What became clear for both of us in that room was that the enemy had established a very clear plan of attack on my life and up until that point it was working. I was broken. I was confused. I felt guilty. I felt hopeless. I was in my mind

a perverted mess well beyond God's grace and that's where
the enemy needed me to be because as long as I stayed there,
I would never walk towards my calling and my purpose.
As you can imagine, I left that day full of emotions, thoughts
and confusion that still to this day brings me to tears
sometimes in my counseling sessions. I've felt angry at my
parents. I've felt angry towards my cousins. I've even felt
angry towards God. To this day, I still struggle to go to my
hometown and to walk into my granddad's house. Though
for years, I decided to stuff those memories back into the
closet and move on, Jesus insisted on holding that pain in
His crucified hands. I didn't see it then but on that day, with
that counselor, sat the Holy Spirit. And in that room,
something *significan't* began to shift in my life.

I don't know where you are as you read this chapter.
I'm not sure of your story or your pain but what I do know
is that you have it. It may not be like mine, it may be a
totally different wound. Maybe your wound isn't even a
childhood wound. Maybe the most devastating thing in your
life happened as an adult. Maybe it wasn't a long time ago,
maybe it was last week. Maybe there's not even another
person on the other side of the wound, maybe you feel like
its God. Either way, the message is the same, Jesus wants
you to come to Him heavy-laden as you may be and allow
Him to hold all of you in His nail pierced hand and receive

the healing that the stripes on His back (Isaiah 53:5) has paid for!

Naming Our Wounds

Jesus knows all about wounds. He understands rejection, abandonment, abuse, injustice and feeling alone. In His life and in His death, Jesus knew our pain. He knew our suffering. Yet, as much as He knew those things, He knew healing. As we read the Gospels in our Bibles we see that Jesus went around with healing on His mind. He healed sicknesses, physical ailments, blinded eyes and broken hearts all as a foreshadowing of His coming Kingdom but also as a picture of what Jesus does for us spiritually when we trust Him.

One of the most fascinating pieces about the healing stories for me is that those in need had no issue in acknowledging their need. In fact, in many cases what they allowed to lead out in their interaction with Jesus was what hurt the worst about their lives. As I think about that, my mind wonders to a sermon I heard recently about anger. In speaking to best practices of dealing with anger the pastor shared that naming it is chief. He explained that when we allow our anger, whether just or unjust, to go unnamed, we leave ourselves open to finding comfort and pleasure in the sin that can flow from the anger. He went on to say instead we should name our anger and give it full acknowledgement because when we do, we invite Jesus to hold it and the Holy Spirit to disciple it. We are forced into the place of decision and must decide if we will choose to crucify Christ or live in His resurrection. If this is true for our anger then I believe it is true for our wounds. When we acknowledge our hurt, our pain and suffering before God and name our need, we in turn invite Jesus to hold and heal it through the work of the Holy Spirit in our lives. We are forced into a place of decision and must the question like the lame man in John 5:6 if "Do you want to be healed?"

What might *signifcan'tly* change about our lives if we knew our wounds, named them and beyond that, committed to the journey of letting God heal them? What strongholds could begin to unravel? What generational cycles would begin to break? What secret sin might become a public testimony of God's grace? What possibilities and quality of life might exist for us on the other side? I guess the answer to those depends on the answer to this, Do you believe Jesus when He said," I have come so that they may have life and have it in abundance?"

To borrow from the style of the Apostle Paul let me say, I do not write as If I have made it to the other side but I press on. What I do know is that, I have acknowledged what existed in the past and what the enemy stole from me. And I daily strain ahead towards the healing in which God's word has promised me in and through Christ Jesus. What I have tasted and seen is enough for me to believe that healing is possible. Strongholds can be broken. Generational cycles will die. Sin will not win and my hope is truly a living one, not just in eternity but for today! The journey as not been easy by any means but I refuse to believe He would bring me this far to not bring me to the other side. If it is true for me, then friend it is true for you!

The Road Ahead

It was almost two years after that counseling session before I took any major steps at healing. I wrestled and grappled with God about the why behind my story and convinced myself I had enough in me to fix it on my own. God in only the way He could through different people, messages and books continued to chip away at my lack of trust in Him. Before long, I realized that a huge part of my way out of a wounded place was not to stuff it but to keep talking about it.

For me, this looked like finally sharing the events of that day with my mom and acknowledging my anger towards her. This looked like sharing it with my wife and acknowledging my shame about it. This looked like sharing it on a stage in a room full of men to model vulnerability. This looked like finding community with a similar story and committing accountability. It even looks like writing about it in this book to preach hope to those still held captive to their wounds. Each has its own purpose but each invites more healing. I share those examples not because they were easy but because they were necessary for me. I needed the relief of complete honesty but also the hope of Godly redemption.

With that, here is my invitation. I invite you to Heal Wholeheartedly. That is to pursue healing with a sincere heart and an unwavering commitment to see it through. Flip every stone and find safe, Godly counsel to walk hand in hand with as you do. Name what hurts about your life. Acknowledge your anger about it and then accept God's promise that if you trust Him with it, what may be a lump of coal in your hands will be a diamond in His. It's never too late and it can never happen too soon for you. HEAL!

Prayer

Father God, I thank you your promise of healing. I thank you that you desire to see me healed not just in eternity but today. I want to know your healing but I need your help. Lord. I acknowledge that sometimes I doubt you and your ability to do for me what you have done for others. I repent of my disbelief and ask that help my unbelief become certainty. Lord, I request that you would meet me where I am weak and be my strength. Where I need to let go, I pray that you would give me courage to release. Give me the capacity to imagine a life where my wounds no longer rule my life. Allow me to know the reality of a healed life.

Holy Spirit, help me to walk obediently towards whatever might be necessary to see this through. I thank you because it's already done. In Jesus' name I pray, Amen

3 Heart Deep Questions

1)   What Did You Hear From God As You Read?

2)   What Did You Learn About Yourself?

3)   Is There A Step You Need to Take? If So, What Does That Look Like?

Chapter 5

Love Sacrificially

"For even the Son of Man did not come to be served, but to serve, and to give his life as a ransom for many." -Mark 10:45

What is love? This is a question that has swirled the minds of every generation as we contemplate this complex reality of our existence as human beings. Love in some way has been at the basis of every catastrophic and catalytic human event throughout the history of time. Love lived wrong or love lived rightly has caused man to work tirelessly towards their desired end since the beginning of time.

There are many verses in the Bible that not only speak about love but also simply display the love of God in his response to His people. Look no further than the hallmark of all Bible verses, John 3:16. God's love for the world is so deep that He went the extra mile and gave Jesus as a loving sacrifice in exchange for our redemption and salvation. That verse speaks of love but in its speaking, also displays its beauty. Yet when I examine that love I walk away feeling its imperfection. Now just to clarify, I am positing imperfection to mean it's against our finite logic. God is perfect and all He does and wills is therefore perfect.

In spite of that truth, the perfection of God to us can sometimes seem questionable at best.

In my finite knowledge and perspective, the idea of giving my son over to an adulterous world for their free rejection or acceptance doesn't sound like the best return of value for my love. Or what about Jesus, the one who had to endure the pain and horror of crucifixion? Out of His love for humanity and obedience to His father, Jesus faithfully did what many of us couldn't fathom. Is love that powerful?

Be More

"Be More" is a go-to phrase for me. I believe it embodies the totality of life and love. If we all simply strived to "be more" than our desires, shortcomings, selfishness, fears and anything else unlovely about us by clinging to Jesus, much of what we read about in our Bibles would happen in our communities.

To speak more on love, I want to share the words to one of my standard wedding sermons with you. What they represent is my best attempt at instilling into a soon-to-be married couple the imperfectly perfect love God is calling them to for the rest of their lives. What it embodies are principles that I want to invite you to embrace for the rest of your life not just for marital bliss, but for all of life and relationship. The words will be framed to call two individuals together but I challenge you to wonder aloud how you might appropriate these principles to invade your love. My words are inspired by Ephesians 4:2-6. Before you continue, stop and take a moment to read those verses for yourself!

In this particular passage Paul is speaking to a group of Christians, instructing them how to live fruitfully in the Body of Christ. The body of Christ is a unique body because it is made up of a bunch of individuals who have been united under the commonality that Jesus is Lord. This one commonality is the wild card that is meant to overcome all the difficulties that would present itself to this body!

After informing them to walk worthy of the calling they have received, he moves to giving simple yet (as we know) hard instructions. He calls them to humility, the call to always be second for the sake of someone else. He calls them to gentleness, not to be confused with being timid, but to have strength under control. He calls them to patience, which is to embrace long-suffering understanding that the best way to stick together is to stick to what matters most, each other. He then moves to telling them to fight for their unity by accepting one another, faults, flaws and all, with love and peace in mind. He closes out this passage of scripture reminding these believers that there is only one body of Christ and that body shares the same spirit, the same hope, the same faith and the same Lord. As you two enter into this most beautiful covenant, allow me to impart a few words to you inspired by this passage:

1) Always Remember Your Calling:

Today, you both enter into a new calling. That calling is to be a faithful and committed spouse! Yet, above that calling is your calling to be children of God and imitators of Christ! As you pursue marital bliss, never forsake the higher calling that holds this one together.

2) Choose Second Place:

The only way to truly live humbly, to truly live gently and to truly live patiently with each other is to first submit to each other. Be the first to say "I love you." Be the first to say "I'm Sorry." Be the first to deny yourself and be the first to build up the other. Choosing second place for yourself is choosing first place for your marriage.

3) Remember Who You Chose

The beautiful thing about marriage is that you two chose each other, and the beautiful thing about a wedding is that you two are publicly committing to choose each other every day for the rest of your lives. Today you are choosing to become one body -- a body bound together by God through and for His glory. If this body is to remain, the way we will bind it today, you must never stop choosing each other first!

4) **Be More**

Be More has become a personal mantra and guiding light for me over the years, and I want to share that with you today. So before God and people you love, I call you two personally to Be More.

I call you to Be More than the man you're used to being, Be More than the woman you are used to being, Be More than a Married couple and Be More than Best Friends.

I call you to Be More Patient, Be More Kind, Be More Humble, Be More Satisfied.

I call you to Be More Honest, Be More Forgiving, Be More Protective, Be More Hopeful.

I call you to Be More Consistent, Be More Trustworthy, Be More Life, and the greatest of these: Be More Love.

As you've likely concluded, love is a hard and intentional thing. We confuse the word so often in our culture with a less meaningful substitute. Love is often centered on how something or someone makes us feel. It can be uttered to express our deep lust and desire for food and companionship alike. Rarely does it live out its full potential and purpose in our lives. Have you ever pondered the idea that the capacity to love was given to us with a purpose and mission in mind?

We would be hard pressed to find any place in scripture that love did not find a companion in tangible action. God's love for us in John 3:16 finds measurable action in the giving of Jesus. Though justice, discipline and judgement is consistently a theme of the Old Testament, there is always a measure of God's love present through action. Whether that action is simply caring for Adam and Eve after their fall or restoring and redeeming a remnant in times of complete rebellion by His people Israel, His love has a tangible action. Even the discourse of Peter and Jesus that we read about in the previous chapter has this factor. Peter was asked a number of times about His love for Jesus, and each time tangible action and mission was the proof. At this point I hope you get the picture, but if not, here is the truth: Love has no better proof than when it builds the life of someone else, instead of yours. Simply put, there is no love without sacrifice! At least no love worth having or one that will last.

As we consider the sacrificial love our position in Christ calls us to, let us remember to rely on the Spirit of God that makes it all possible in this life. Jesus said in John 15:5 that we could do nothing apart from Him so a self-effort based love is not the call here. Instead, we are compelled by a Christ-centered love. A love that remembers Jesus also said, "Anything is possible with God", even loving difficult people. I don't know where your love meter is right now. I don't know who you need to love in "spite of" today but I challenge you to say yes. Truth is, *significan't* love is sometimes love we can't imagine, but it remains love we are called to give. Sometimes it's hard love. It can be self-denying love. It's love over and beyond ourselves, it's a love that mirrors Jesus! Yeah, it can be bitter at first but a bitter obedience is better than a bitter heart. Love sacrificially!

Prayer

Father God, I thank you for your unfailing and faithful love. I thank you that your love sacrificially found me in my lowest place and saved me, while I was your enemy. I desire to love those in my life and in my influence, the way that you first loved me. I acknowledge that on my own, I can't do it, so I humbly ask you to help me walk this path. I repent of where I've fallen short or missed the mark. I repent of anytime that I've resisted your nudge to give what I get freely from you. With that I ask for your help. Holy Spirit, help me make much of Jesus by the way that I love beyond excuses. Help me to display your fruit as I walk out the gospel tangibly in my life. In Jesus' name I pray, Amen

3 Heart Deep Questions

1) What Did You Hear From God As You Read?

2) What Did You Learn About Yourself?

3) Is There A Step You Need to Take? If So, What Does That Look Like?

Chapter 6

Give Unthinkably

"Don't neglect to do what is good and to share, for God is pleased with such sacrifices."- Hebrews 13:16

There is no doubt that the idea of giving has taken on a nefarious subtlety in the realm of the church world. With the history of televangelists soliciting money for blessing in modern history or the Middle-Ages Catholic church practice of selling indulgences for forgiveness of sin, I don't blame people who hate to hear their pastor talk about giving or money. As I look back with adult eyes, I remember my own scars about this.

For a short time when I was a kid, we attended a newer church plant where the pastor had big dreams for "his" ministry (as he called it from time to time). I remember multiple occasions when the time came to hear God's word, those who listened got what now sounds like a sales pitch and sometimes, an ultimatum. On one occasion, he used his sermon time to chastise the church for not giving enough money so now his family had to sleep in the cold with no heat. Now our church had about 50 members including kids, with 90% of the adults being single moms or elderly women, so the idea that this batch wasn't giving enough to support his family didn't sit right with me, even as a 10-year-old kid. As I look back, I graciously want to attribute that time to his youthful vision and an unbridled expectation or maybe even needing more preparation for the hard work of church planting. Regardless, I'm thankful my mom finally got the vision to leave that place. She was new to committed faith so it took a while to discern, but I guess after other "alleged" improprieties arose, it became clear we should leave.

As I write that story, I feel myself getting angry. I get angry at the wickedness that exists among God's people at times. I get angry at how manipulation and fear can always somehow swindle us. But I also get angry because stories like that happen all the time and for many people, they don't rebound like my family. They simply leave the church for good, never to trust it again.

Mom

In spite of that story being true, I sometimes marvel at my mom's resilience. Though at the time she was swooped into the madness of what I will call a scheme, it didn't destroy her theology of giving. As we moved to our next church, I saw mom time and time again find ways to, in her words, "plant seeds" in her giving from the little we had towards the ministry of God. I count myself extremely blessed to have witnessed my own version of the widow's mite in what I will call the "single mother's mite."

Sometimes with the gas light on and the light bill due, mom still gave unthinkably. Without her knowing it, her conviction to trust God with her giving was allowing me to witness God's faithfulness in real time. Sure we were still poor and found ourselves on food stamps from time to time. Sure there were times when my only real meal was at school, but I never thought God wasn't faithful because mom kept giving and God kept providing.

The biggest moment for this witness was after my mom almost lost her life in a car wreck, you guessed it, coming from church. It was a rainy night but mom was faithful to drive the 35 minutes to our church that Wednesday evening. For the first time ever, she told me I didn't have to go but could stay home. What I thought was my mom being cool, I now count as God being gracious to me. Church started at 6pm and it always went long so I didn't expect her until around 9pm. Well 9pm quickly became 11pm before I received word that my mom had been in a bad car wreck and was in the hospital. After flying through the windshield, losing her scalp on the way, she broke her leg in multiple places. She had survived multiple rolls in our vehicle, which was totaled. The damage was so bad that she was unrecognizable and would eventually be on bedrest for over a year.

For a single-parent family this meant we would lose everything. My mom had a typical factory job that required manual labor, so that was lost. Our home, which she was striving to pay off on her own after my stepfather's infidelity, was eventually lost so we had no place to live. Luckily my brother was away at college but I became a nomad, bouncing from house to house with family members until one of my aunts took me in for good. In a matter of weeks we went from a family getting by, to a family with nothing. As tragic as that moment was, triumphant was my mom's faith in who *God* was. In the next couple years as my mom worked towards getting her mobility back, what she lacked in resources she gave in her encouragement. Time and time again, she "planted seeds" with her words proclaiming God's goodness and pouring into me and others confidence and strength. I still remember Christmas that year when somehow without any means, she still managed to get me a game console. It was an old one but it meant the world to me because I knew she had to have literally saved pennies for months and months to get that $100 game for me. She couldn't help but give; it was unthinkable then and is still unthinkable now.

After working her whole adult life, my mom applied for disability and was denied multiple times without an actual opportunity to state her case. On a walker and still pretty much bedridden she kept her giving spirit. Finally after two years applying, she was approved. What this meant was that the state owed her and her children back pay for the time they denied her unjustly. Weeks later, she started to receive her monthly support and I received a check for over $10,000. The kicker to my receiving this check was that it came in the mail as I was on my way to college orientation. As a broke kid going off to college, there was no better timing for this than that moment. As I cried tears of joy for what that money would mean for me as I went off to college, I couldn't help but recall all the times my single mother gave her mite. She had given unthinkably in my opinion for so many years and here was God doing the same for me.

As I recall it, we cashed the check when I got home and the first thing I did with that money was take 10% and give unthinkably back to God at my church that Sunday morning. As a 17-year-old kid who had never held more than $100, here I was without pause giving close to $1,500 to a church offering. I never thought twice about it. I think mama modeled pretty well for me that it was God's money anyway

Matt and Kristy

About 9 years ago as a young family, my wife and I moved away from our college town to kick off our life together. After living in a terrible apartment for a year, we decided we would buy a home. At the time, I was a state law enforcement officer and my wife was a preschool teacher so we qualified for some cool programs for first-time home buyers. As we went through this process, we were simultaneously searching for a church home. We had thought we found a place but soon I began to sniff out similar patterns from that childhood church that scarred me, so for several weeks we church hopped. In the midst of that church hopping I had the chance to meet Matt, who is now one of my best friends and someone my kids know as Uncle.

Coach Robison, as I knew him then, was a local high school wrestling coach whom I had reached out to about helping with the team. He was gracious and agreed to meet with me. During our first conversation in the McDonald's inside a Wal-Mart, of all places (*if you knew Matt this would make total sense*), I discovered he was a wrestling coach who had never wrestled and I was a former wrestler who wanted to coach; and he was a pastor planting a church and I was a churchgoer looking for a home. This just felt God-ordained! Over the next month or so my wife and I, along with our 6 month old son, visited the church. They were still meeting in a movie theatre and oftentimes Chris Brown would kick on mid-sermon to let us know it was time to go. We didn't like it at first but we went back a couple times.

In our time of testing out the church, our housing contract fell through two days before closing and our apartment lease was up the week after we had planned to close. We were reassured the issue could be fixed quickly and we would likely be delayed two weeks. With that in mind, we lived out our last week in the apartment and made plans to move into an extended stay motel until we could close. It was not ideal and our minds could only imagine the potentially terrible things that had previously happened at this place but it would have to do. Like clockwork, the night we moved in, Matt invited us over for dinner at their home. As we were having dinner, he casually mentioned he saw we were living at a motel. Apparently my wife had spilled the beans on Facebook that day and he had seen it. As I began to explain the circumstances, he cut me off and said, "Y'all aren't staying at a motel. We have an extra room, y'all can just stay here." (Hopefully you read that in your best southern)

In hearing the offer, I politely declined the offer, thinking in my head how crazy they were to think we would move in with them. This was the first white dinner table we had ever been invited to, and now we were supposed to move in? As dinner finished and we were leaving, he made the offer again and we declined. As we drove back to our decked-out extended stay, I could feel my wife tensing up as we drew closer. All of a sudden she blurted out, "Call Pastor Matt and tell him we are coming. I'm not sleeping at an extended stay when someone has offered us a better spot!" Apparently, my attempt to warm up the room with some of our belongings hadn't convinced my wife to stop her imagination from venturing to all the true crime shows she watched. So full of pride and fear, I called Matt and asked if we could come. Of course he said yes, so we packed up and went. It was only going to be a week. What harm could it do, I thought?

Well, a week turned into a month and a month turned into three and before you know it, two failed closings later we had lived with Matt and his family for six months! What started off as an unthinkable giving up of their comfort by inviting a family into their space for a week, turned into an even more unthinkable giving six months later. As a dude who grew up in a town in which white people never crossed over our side of the tracks, it made no sense to my mind that this family from all places, Kentucky, would be so welcoming and giving to us. Just as my mom had shown me what giving looked like in her way, Matt and his wife Kristy, showed us what giving looks like with their lives. Those six months for us were monumental in who we are as people today. Because of their giving, I got to witness a Christian man leading his family up close and personal for the first time. Because of their giving, I was able to imagine a more beautiful life and existence that included deep, intimate relationship with people who didn't look like me. Because of their giving, I was able to face my pornography addiction as a young believer as Matt pastored but most of all friended me through confession and repentance. Because of their giving, I was able to take my mom's lessons on planting seeds and extend that to the whole of my life. I was able to see that giving actually begins with how you live your life for others. Quite frankly, I would not be a pastor today or currently live in Kentucky (go figure), had Matt and Kristy not so graciously offered us a week's stay at their home. Over those months, we didn't just live there but we were discipled there. They spoke into our lives. We were given words of affirmation and exhortation. We were challenged and prayed over. Ultimately, we were sent out to give as we had been so graciously given.

For the sake of chapter length, I will simply say this: part of giving unthinkably is first understanding that you have *received* unthinkably. Both my mom and the Robisons knew that to be true and lived their lives in such a way that it shaped the people around them. They aren't perfect people by any means but by the power of the Spirit, they are "giving people." And giving people is what the *significan't* life calls us to be. Forgiveness is given. Reconciliation requires giving. Love is a gift and without growth, our selfishness will give us every reason not to give. I mean, when we think about it, our entire faith hinges on the idea that God gives unthinkably so that we receive unmeasurably. Through the example of Jesus, we are called to be those who give our lives to the glory of God and lay them down for our loved ones and neighbors.

In The Gospel of Luke chapter 14, Jesus makes a claim that has for generations, moved people to this type of life when he says this: *"Whoever does not bear his own cross and come after me cannot be my disciple."*–Luke 14:27

Words as such, have a way in finding the deepest pockets of our souls and realign our priorities. They exegete our hearts and serve as a reminder of what our lives are truly all about. Jesus bore His own cross for the sake of humanity and the call for those who follow Him is to go and do likewise in our lives daily. When we do so, we bring His kingdom here and make moments we hear others talk about, in our own lives.

In this chapter, I bragged about people I love, who gave unthinkably to me. I could have gone on and told you about folks like Aunt Nora and Uncle Sam. The Hamner family, Coach Davis, Dickey and Miller. Mr. Veal or my Seventh Grade teacher Mrs. Foy. All people who left an undoubtable mark on my life but then this chapter would be too long. Instead I want to pivot to you and allow the stories here to serve as a step stool for your own. They are here to serve as tangible examples of what our lives can produce when we walk with the Spirit and allow Him to do what He wants with who we are and what we have. It's what life can look like when we stop focusing on how we might get burned but instead on how God might be glorified. Not just from our excess but from our reserves. Not just from our money but from our lives. Not for the recognition but for His mission and His Kingdom. If that type of giving doesn't represent your life then the question is where can you start? To whom or to what in your sphere of influence can you begin to give unthinkably? Where have you been nudged in the past to give and have not done so yet? May I give you some advice you likely won't regret? Go for it, Give!

Prayer

Father God, I thank you for the way you give. I thank you that you give in such a way that sometimes I can't describe it...My heart desires to give as you do but I need your help. In saying that, I ask that you would fill me with your compassion and mercy. Fill me with your vision to see how I might be one who gives to those around me. I repent of times I turn my eyes in convenience from your open doors to give. Holy Spirit, help me make much of Jesus by the way that I give beyond my own thinking. Lead me towards streams of righteousness as I seek to do justice, walk humbly and love mercy every day of my life.

In Jesus' name I pray, Amen

3 Heart Deep Questions

1) What Did You Hear From God As You Read?

2) What Did You Learn About Yourself?

3) Is There A Step You Need to Take? If So, What Does That Look Like?

Chapter 7

Repent Consistently

"Therefore repent and turn back, so that your sins may be wiped out."-Acts 3:19

If there was ever something that I believe has escaped the reality of the American church, its repentance. Repentance is the idea of trading our way of sin for the way of Christ. Repentance is something you do. It's something you say. It's something you pursue. Repentance is internal and external. It's soul deep and physically tangible. It's a one-time fix and an everyday practice. It's moment by moment and reaches into the past. It is a complex yet simple spiritual discipline that impacts all facets of life. It precedes forgiveness and reconciliation. It is driven by love and growth and if you ask Zacchaeus, see Luke 11, it can look like reaching deep and giving to others what is due to them.

Unfortunately, it seems the idea of repentance has been reduced to "moment in time" opportunities in the church. They're the moments that organizations and denominations use to confess what the rest of us already know. They're the moments in time that pastors guilty of infidelity use to confess what has already been exposed. Those are the moments that most define repentance in the

American church context. It seems year after year, one of our faith heroes falls from grace with a statement of repentance as she or he heads out the door. It seems year after year denominations, institutions and churches have come out with statements acknowledging their history of racism or some form of sexual abuse, only to ask the greater church at large to not lose confidence in them. In a weird way, it seems repentance has become more about acceptance from man versus rightness with God. It has become more about saving face rather than renewing our vows with our covenant savior Jesus Christ.

Now in saying that, I do want to acknowledge my appreciation for a corporate perspective of sin and repentance. It is always refreshing to see Christians acknowledge our familial nature in such an individualized faith world. Yet if those official statements and position papers are not birthed from a room of broken people humbled before God, grieving of the sin it confesses, then the statements and papers are nothing more than words and carry no more legitimacy than a Russian bot posting American political trash on Facebook.

I believe our infatuation with grace and the beautiful doctrine that flows from it has unknowingly numbed our generation to the pursuit of holiness. We have so much comfort and systematic clarity in a God of sovereignty and grace that we have no frame of reference for His justice, wrath and discipline. We forfeit all the ministry of the wrestling therein to the cross of Jesus as a catch all for our daily responsibility to walk humbly and holy before a great God.

Just as relationship with Jesus invites us into *significan'tce* in our love, forgiveness and reconciliation, it also invites us in the same way to a long stare in the mirror of our hearts, minds and actions. It invites us to a Holy Spirit led honesty with ourselves that makes pulling the log out of our eye more comfortable than keeping it in place. But before we can ever get to that point we must feel the weight again of our brokenness and of our sin. We must revisit the many Proverbs that remind us to walk in integrity and the many Psalms that remind us of the cost of choosing otherwise. We must acknowledge its impact and the damage it does. We must grow weary of the cover-up work we engage in daily and embrace the better and narrower way of life.

One of my favorite preachers to listen to is the late Dr. Gardner Taylor. Dr. Taylor is a legend in the preaching world so he obviously said many great things over his lifetime. In one particular message I heard years ago, he broached the subject of sin. Being a reverend in the New York area with opportunities to lecture all over the city, Dr. Taylor had heard the rumblings that sin was a word that had grown tired on people and the subject had passed its age. In the face of that criticism Dr. Taylor acknowledged the idea that the word in itself might have lost its luster on the consciousness of people, but its impact still had a grip on our world. Speaking to his moment in time, he pointed to the Vietnam War where many of our strongest and brightest were dying. He pointed to the failing schools and inequities back home that were plaguing communities. He pointed to the growing drug problems in America that were ravishing a generation. He pointed to the increasing divorce rates and infidelity that was destroying families and declared that though some may be tired of *hearing* about sin, we had better grow tired of sin itself and what it is doing to our society, to our world and to our families.

Minus the Vietnam War reference, might I insert the same urgency for us? The beginning of that urgency is confessing the ugliness within and the sinful works of our hands. Now I can admit, confessing sin can feel as shocking as keeping a food diary. Once you get it out there, you feel awful, but feeling awful in both of those cases is a catalyst to feeling great later. If we could just grow comfortable sitting at the feet of Jesus and giving more than our blanket statements of repentance, we would truly see how sweet grace is. If we could embrace heart-deep evaluation and confession, we would find it easier to follow the invitations we've covered so far in this book.

Two Types of Repentance

As we continue this chapter, I want to hone in on two areas of repentance, first personal and then communal. One would be hard pressed to read the Bible and not come away with a sound theology on personal confession and repentance. In my mind, it would take a willful blind eye to miss the implicit examples of what confession and repentance before God looks like. I think of people like Isaiah who confessed His unclean lips or I think of David and his heart in Psalm 32, or better yet Psalm 51, where he pleads for mercy from a God of unfailing love. I even think of Job who by all accounts showed great trust and perseverance in the face of trial, repented in dust and ashes. Beyond that, our New Testaments are littered with stories of repentance both for salvation and restoration with God.

One of my favorite examples is found in the life of the Apostle Paul when the Bible records him as Saul. Saul was a man most would easily consider committed to his faith. From what we know about him, he would be what we might consider Sunday school teacher material. He was well learned and versed in the Torah and Jewish practices. Beyond that, Saul had great zeal for the God revealed in our Old Testaments. Yet in the face of a new movement of God, Saul, in what he understood to be faithfulness, stood against and openly opposed Christ and His subsequent movement... so much so that our Bibles tell us he essentially became a bounty hunter of Christians to ensure they were punished for what he thought to be blasphemy. Yet if you know the story, you know something *significan't* happened in his life. While on his most audacious journey yet, Saul was met by a light from Heaven that we know to be Jesus. In this moment, Saul was confronted with his sin. Then in the way only God can through a series of events, Saul's life and mission were transformed from one that pursued Christians for death to one that pursued people in Christ *saving* them from death! If you haven't caught it yet, repentance is a powerful practice. I believe one of the reasons Saul's story is there is to display to us what might be possible in our lives if we were to embrace this practice ourselves. What dead things might come to life if we would commit to daily repentance and to stop persecuting the Christ in us? How would our individual commitment to walking in integrity before God improve our ability to do so before our spouses, children and neighbors? What things might we feel more qualified to walk towards if we had a practice of truly being known by God?

The Bible tells us in Ephesians 4 that by our sin grieves the Holy Spirit. It reminds us that the very way we choose to live has the power to grieve the God in us, yet because we have a nature contrary to holiness Romans 8 invites us to allow that very same Spirit of God to intercede for us in our weakness. It's having eyes to see the error of our ways. It's having the courage to admit them to be true for our lives. And it's the humility and the resistance of pride to ask for help understanding where we are deficient. Plainly put, an essential part of embracing a *significan't* life for ourselves is embracing the *significan't* help of God to repent and resist consistently.

Communal Repentance

Now, as it works, where we are being most consistent in our personal lives has a way of overflowing into our community. One of the most amazing yet sometimes most difficult parts of the Christian life is that it is a communal one. In the western church, we have worked really hard to individualize our faiths. I don't believe this is intentional as much as it is a product of our individualized culture, especially here in America. To combat this, it takes hard work for the Christian to recapture the familial reality of our faith.

When our New Testaments opens, John the Baptist is baptizing those who are repentant into a communal redirection. When the gentiles received the gospel, they were grafted into God's special people. And one day when Christ returns, He will redeem for Himself a bride and a church that covers the span of time and the tribe, tongues and nations of the world. This shift has the power to reshape much of how we operate in our faith. It moves us from an individual responsibility to a collective one. It moves us from only focusing on our sins to the sins of our Christ community. It allows us to see and own the sins of our family, our ancestors and those we are bound to in Christ.

Let's revisit Saul for a second. After his individual conversion, the Bible tells us Saul began to immediately preach that Jesus was the Son of God in the synagogues. Effectively, Saul was taking responsibility for the collective sin of the people and calling his beloved faith family and community to repentance. His individual repentance unleashed him to a communal one.

Now as I write that, I am keenly aware of what might be coming to your mind. I am in no way advocating for you or anyone else to go and scream at your church, family or friends about their sin. What Saul did was decent and in order with the customs of the synagogue so in the same way, we are to conduct ourselves. Yet, what I am calling you to is a practice of carrying the weight of our collective sin and shortcomings with you in your prayer closet, to repent on behalf of Christ's bride. I am charging you to have eyes to see and ears to hear where we are not being faithful to the mission of Jesus in our churches and communities. I am calling you to be brokenhearted by those things. I am inviting you to grieve with the Holy Spirit about it. I am encouraging you to first repent on your knees on our behalf and then with the help of the Holy Spirit, move your feet to help change our direction where you can.

Walking Out Repentance

One major truth we learn from the life of Paul is that there is no such thing as repentance without action. Where we pray for God to move, we commit to walk hand in hand with Him to see it through. In one of my Master's degree courses, my professor posed a question in regard to Luke 2:52 where we are told Jesus in His youth grew in knowledge, size and favor among God and man. His question was this: Where is the Church at large growing the best and subsequently the least if these were categories to consider. Immediately my brain went to knowledge as the strength, simply based on the brilliant scholars of our day and all the resources at our disposal. We know and have more today than might be for our own good. And when it came to the least, well I found it quite easy to say "favor with man" when it came to the communal nature of our faith. I pointed out that I attend and serve in an Evangelical context and for the most part, I've learned that Evangelical has become like a curse word in the eyes of men in recent years. Because of our unrepentant nature when it comes to various racial, communal and social issues in and outside of our walls, we have much work to do to regain the credibility and trust of minorities and those outside the faith. I guess another way of saying that, is because we haven't heeded the words of Paul to walk wisely among outsiders, or the words of Peter to always be ready to give an account, the church has actually become a hindrance to the work of Christ. I would contend that because we have forsaken our commitment to repentance, the very vessel meant to reach the world could very well be turning it away.

Unrepentance Has Consequences

What if I told you some in the church are killing the work of black and minority churches because of public defiance and political affinity? The biggest apologetic work in black and minority communities today is convincing people that Christianity isn't the white man's religion. Why is that? It's because we have yet to collectively repent for our Europeanized Jesus portraits and among other things, the use of our faith to further enslave. We simply call for unity without ownership of the past.

What if I told you that some Christians are turning away neighbors, coworkers and family because of ungodly social media posts and his/her commitment to a yard sign? Just reflect on the unrepentant year of 2020 and unapologetic year of 2021 for proof. While there are some who have faithfully used their platforms to challenge and edify the church, many have simply boldly participated in the chaos, all while proclaiming Jesus as Lord. Some were even convinced Jesus commissioned them towards their divisive behaviors as they grossly misuse scriptures to condemn, criminalize and harass others.

As I reflect on those truths, I most regret how pastors and leaders have contributed to this problem. I reflect on how many have removed the topics of and even the words "sin and repentance" from their pulpits and tool bags of ministry. We instead opt for softer words like "struggle, mistakes and hard seasons" missing the hearts that are not simply prone to wonder but do so willingly. Now in saying that, I don't mean we should bring back "fire and brimstone" or "turn or burn" preaching but we do need authoritatively honest shepherding to emerge again. We need the same Spirit that carried the prophets of old to fill our sermons, bible studies and books again to call God's people to a greater *significan'tce*. Repentance isn't fun because it requires that we admit we are sinners but take hope because Jesus said, to those very people is the Kingdom of Heaven! If you ask me, that a good deal! I say this to myself as I say it to you friend, Repent and do it often!

Prayer

Father God, I thank you for being a God of unmerited favor and second chances. I thank you that you welcome me in my broken state back into your presence daily. My heart desires to repent as you would call me to but I need your help. In saying that, I ask that you would break me down so that you might build me up. Give me eyes to see and ears to hear where you are calling me away from my sin and into your safety. Holy Spirit, help me make much of my daily opportunities to repent and walk in integrity before God. Bring me to a more complete view of what it means to repent, not only from me but for my family, my church, my community and this world. Father, I repent before you today! Thank you for your forgiveness! In Jesus' name I pray, Amen.

3 Heart Deep Questions

1) What Did You Hear From God As You Read?

2) What Did You Learn About Yourself?

3) Is There A Step You Need to Take? If So, What Does That Look Like?

Chapter 8

Pray Persistently

"Rejoice always, pray constantly, give thanks in everything; for this is God's will for you in Christ Jesus."
- 1 Thessalonians 5:16-18

In this last invitation, I want to broach the topic of perhaps one of the most confusing, complex and for some people, awkward parts of the faith: prayer. Prayer has a way of eluding us much like the Holy Spirit in understanding its intent and purpose. Depending on our backgrounds and what we were taught and observed, Christians may approach prayer very differently.

For some, prayer is their soundboard to God, letting Him know everything that is wrong in their lives in hope of convincing Him to move. For others, prayer is their power. For some people this is a belief that they have power to change things with their prayers, and for others it's a belief that prayer is their source of strength; it's their best weapon and encouragement in the difficulty of life. I've been to churches where people prayed loud and long and I've been to others where people pray quiet and short. I've prayed for people and I've seen people prayed over. I've experienced prayers for healing and prayers for protection. I've read them in the Bible and I have even included them in every chapter of this book.

As I write this, my desire is not to debate and give my theological perspective on prayer. In short I believe prayer changes things, but I also believe prayer changes us! The more we are willing to go to God in prayer, the more we realize where we fall short, where we need help and where to place our faith. In Jesus' ministry we have a few examples of Him teaching on prayer but also simply Him modeling prayer for us. In Luke 11 we see Jesus teaching His disciples how to pray. This is where we get the Lord's Prayer, which can be heard in locker rooms nationwide, before people board planes and all sorts of other places. In our tradition, this prayer has become a catch all of acknowledging God and maybe for some, a way to get a little favor from Him. I can admit, in my younger years that might have been my thought, but today as I look back on that passage, I find a much more robust understanding and appreciation. What I am most drawn to are two invitations I believe we receive from Jesus in regard to prayer: **1) Come to God as His child and 2) Be persistent.**

Our Father

Jesus begins His teaching on prayer with the encouragement that His disciples should pray in this way, "Our Father." This sometimes subtle but substantial instruction carries many implications that we cannot bear to miss. A father is one who originates and gives life. Father speaks to headship, intimacy and relationship. It speaks to the role of care and instruction. It speaks to responsibility. In Jesus' instruction, He is reminding the disciples and us of those life-giving truths. Many people flame out on a persistent prayer life because they've approached it with the wrong posture and privilege. Oftentimes, people can find themselves approaching God in prayer like a genie. We make a wish and He answers. The problem with this is that God is not subject to us. So when God doesn't grant our wishes like some blue genie, we are left filling in the gaps with our finite and sinful assumptions.

Some approach God in fear. There is something to having a healthy fear and reverence for God but it's another thing entirely when that fear hinders our relationship with a loving God. Beyond those, there are a bevy of other incomplete, inconsistent or downright wrong views of God and prayer that pull Christ-followers away from persistence in prayer. In spite of all the options, Jesus invites us into a rich and worthy communion with the Father in our prayers. In the way that a three-year-old meets daddy at the door after work, we are invited to meet the Father in our prayers. In the way that a child goes to their parent dependent, we too are invited to go to our Father dependent. Persistent prayer will never make sense until we make sense of our need for our Father and how He wholly wants to meet our needs.

Persistence

After we know our need, we find freedom to walk in them persistently hand in hand with our Heavenly Father. Later in His explanation of prayer (Luke 11), Jesus moves to telling a parable about a persistent friend in need of bread. This man, unashamedly and in persistence, makes his need known to his friend on the other side of the door. We find that because of this persistence and confident boldness, his need was met. After wrapping up that story, Jesus moves to giving more instruction. He invites the disciples to be those who ask, seek and knock when it comes to their prayers. Once again, we see a pattern that calls us to pray like we actually mean it; to pray in such a way that our spiritual feet are moving toward seeking out God. It's also a reminder that as children of God, we are always welcome to bug our Father for what we need because He's a good Father who provides. In a matter of a few lines, Jesus says enough to radically reshape any underwhelming expectation for prayer to one worth salivating over. Many people have put down prayer on account of a wrong theology of prayer. Jesus invites us here to pick it back up. Through His teaching to the disciples, we are invited to pursue a persistence in relationship with the Father because from our persistence in relationship that includes prayer, we find that God provides for our needs.

As I contemplate that story, I think of my household dynamic in 2020 and early 2021. At the time my wife and I had three biological kids of our own with a new one about 8 months away. Like crazy people in love with Jesus, we decided to say yes to fostering during a worldwide pandemic and welcomed two toddlers into our home. We are no saints for doing this, though I believe our sanity should be tested. What a journey that time was! Yet as I say that, I smile thinking of the persistence of the little girl who moved into our home and stole our hearts.

On the first day of arrival, things went about as expected. The kids showed up and were skeptical but because we had our own toddler and other kiddos, they loosened up really quickly. Everybody loved everybody except this little girl when she saw me coming. I wasn't keen to her full story and what her experiences had been but it was clear that my male presence scared and triggered her. I remember night after night of me rocking her to sleep as she slapped and clawed at me to let her go. I remember the immediate tears that filled her eyes as I approached. As time passed and I persistently approached her with a fatherly love, I began to see her walls of protection fall. It took weeks but eventually things began to move in the opposite direction. One diaper change here, one fun bath time there made all the difference. Beyond that, we both have an unhealthy love for snack foods that found many cookies in both our hands as we shared their goodness. In a profound yet subtle way, day by day, through my love she was beginning to reshape her view of men and ultimately began to understand my role as Father in that season of her life. If we fast forward the story just a couple months, you would find a little girl who didn't have words yet but came to me persistently and in boldness. She quite literally on a daily basis followed me around the house for hours tapping my leg for her needs. Sometimes it was just a snuggle and kiss on the cheek. Sometimes she wanted my snack. Other times she wanted to play or needed a diaper change. All in all, she had learned the art of persistence with her foster dad that got her needs met day by day. Though she was always technically dependent on my care for her, she learned to willingly live there, in fact she thrived there.

That story is true, but I invite you to hear it as a parable for your own life. If you do not know God from a place of dependency and persistence--in the same way that toddler now knows me--how might your life be different if you did? What false truths, baggage, trauma and disappointments are robbing you of a deeper prayer life shaped by persistence? What will it take for you to not only pursue but believe in a day in and day out prayer life with God? What do you have to surrender? What needs to be shaped? What needs to be let go? These are all questions worth the wrestling required to resolve. The fact of the matter is, nothing else that you've read up to this point will find any power or any possibility without first accepting this invitation from the "I Can't" place of *significan'tce*. We need persistent prayer and persistent reliance on the Spirit as we seek to live lives that give love and share joy. We need lives dependent on a good Father to live in peace and walk in patience. We need to understand who we are in Christ to display grace-filled kindness and goodness to the world. We need to rely on more than just ourselves to be people who walk out faithfulness with gentleness and self-control. We can't be *significant* without first saying I Can't!

　　　As we wrap up our time together, I want to invite you to reflect. Instead of giving you my hand-written prayer to pray, I invite you to sit still with God for a little bit. I invite you to craft your own, personal prayer that expresses your heart in the face of all you've read. I invite you to be honest and true to yourself before God. Thinking through some of these topics can be hard. They can bring up old wounds and speak to things buried deep. Bring those things to God in prayer! I know some of what you've read might speak directly to where you find yourself today; bring those things to God in prayer! As I stated in the beginning, my goal was to send you away reflective. I have provided space for you to do that on the next few pages but if what I have is not enough, grab your journal or notebook and write it there. As you take time to do this, I believe my seven invitations will only be the doorway to many more that God will send your way as you pursue this everyday life of *significant'ce*! May God join you in your thoughts and prayers!

Prayer Prompt: Reflect

Prayer Prompt: Request

Prayer Prompt: Respond

Doxology

"Holy You Are"

One of my favorite traditions I remember from the little A.M.E. church we attended from time to time in my childhood was the singing of the Doxology. What I loved most was the way that we sang the word "amen" in a long stretched out unison that probably should be spelled like, "aaaaaaameeeeeeen!" As I got older and found myself in a Presbyterian Church (P.C.A) this tradition found me again but this time, I loved it for a different reason. Of course the nostalgia of childhood brought a smile to my face but more than anything, the words and their meaning now made sense to me. Now my delight wasn't found in the swaggerish way it seemed we sang the word "amen." In fact, this congregation didn't sing it that way. No, my delight was found in giving praise and honor to my living God who had saved my life and brought all the *significan'tce* I could ever imagine to me freely. In that respect, the words of the traditional Doxology are still my favorite words to sing.

As a church, we sang those words after receiving from God in the preceding service the reminder of His blessing and the impartation of His word. Beyond that, we sang it as an offering to God before we received our benediction to go and be light to our community. In honor of that sacred tradition, I want to invite you to partake in the Doxology of this book. I don't expect you to sing, though you can if you would like. Ultimately, I want to give you one final invitation to honor the reality of God with words of praise.

Glory to you, nothing of me. Poured out your mercy, your Grace is our peace. Father of love, redeemer and king. Son on a cross, by His blood we are free. Open our hearts, cast out our fears. Jesus before us, guide us as you will. We've seen your power, witnessed your ways. Sovereign and sweet, by grace your love displayed.

Holy, Holy, Holy you are. Holy, Holy, Holy, our God.
Holy, Holy, Holy you are. Holy, Holy, Holy, our God.
Holy, Holy, Holy you are. Holy, Holy, Holy, our God.
Holy, Holy, Holy you are. Holy, Holy, Holy, our God

I believe that the lamb was slain for me. I believe in the lion's victory. I believe that the tomb was empty and that King Jesus will come again! Praise the Father, Praise the Son, Praise the Holy Ghost. May our praise on Earth join His Heavenly Host! May our lives here below reflect His gospel hope! Amen. Amen. And Amen.

Benediction

Dear Friend, may Christ live in your hearts by faith and keep you rooted in His love. May your resting there help you understand all God is and all of what He has for you. When your pursuit of Christ-like significan'tce gets tough, may the Spirit grant you the strength to endure beyond what you thought was able. Where you fall short, fall in His grace and where you reap sorrow, reach for Him and try again. Go in His Peace. Go in His Grace. Go in His Mercy. Go in His Strength. Amen

If you made it here, I say thank you for allowing me to journey with you! I do not take it lightly that God allows me to pastor people through my words. If this book blessed you in any way, do me a favor and share it with others. Sibling in Christ, I may not know you but I love you! May God's peace and grace find you daily as we await His Glorious return! God bless next time, let's sit down around a seltzer, sugar-free of course. It's on me!

Your Friend, Terrence.

55224787R00055